BLACK A]

A BOOK OF POEMS

By

ELINOR WYLIE

With an Essay by

MARTHA
ELIZABETH JOHNSON

First published in 1923

British Library Cataloguing-in-Publication Data
A catalogue record for this book is available
from the British Library

For
W. R. B

LIFE OF ELINOR WYLIE

AN ESSAY BY
MARTHA ELIZABETH JOHNSON, 1936

The work of no poet has achieved fame in such a short time as that of Elinor Wylie. Her growth has been like a series of steps taken in rapid strides, each one carrying her a little higher than the proceeding one. She seems to have emerged from a background of no preparation into a vast field of poetry, as a full—fledged poet.

She produced, in an unbelievably short time, four volumes of poetry and four prose, and these books have placed her among the most accomplished of American poets. These books were all written within a period of eight years; none before her thirty—fourth year and none after her forty—second, which was the year of her death.

She was born Elinor Hoyt. She came from a brilliant American family of English origin and was reared with every social advantage, making her debut in Washington society at the age of twenty. In 1907, when twenty—one, she was married to Phil Hichborn, son of Rear Admiral Hichborn of the United States Navy. This marriage was broken up because of her elopement with Horace Wylie, to whom she was later married after her second elopement with him. At the time of her death she was the wife of William Rose Benet, the poet.

As a girl she loved literature and wrote some poetry when she was eight years of age. Much of her background of classical reading she got in her childhood while living with her parents at Washington. From fourteen to twenty—two she wrote poetry but not really in earnest and then stopped writing for seven years while she was having her escapades and going through the aftermath that made her want to withdraw from public view.

She went to England to live but to the surprise of those who knew her, she soon returned, and the following poem appeared:

> Now why should I, who walk alone,
> Who am ironical and proud,
> Turn when a woman casts a stone,
> At a beggar in a shroud?

She could not adjust herself to her home in England and she did not desire to return to Washington. She was unhappy, alone and unoccupied, so she decided to go to Maine. There she lived alone with her typewriter in a small room over a grocery store, in 1919, and wrote verse that resounded with a sad and mournful note. She had given up a life of luxury and excitement to live in this way and it has been questioned whether

> "It was life's enrichments or life's deprivation that tempted her to write."

Here in Maine she was inspired by the woods and by the sea, but she was dissatisfied — restless — and after a short time she went to New York where she settled down to writing in all earnestness, in her thirty—fourth year. She was probably inspired by her last husband, Mr Benet, the writer, to write with the powerful determination that produced great results. So we find her at the age of thirty—four just discovering the literary gift that was here, after she had been through the most tragic experience, which probably was the thing necessary to call it forth.

Her first published poems appeared in *The Century Magazine,* in *Poetry* and in *The New Republic.* There were some poems she classed as *Incidental Numbers* written in 1921, which was a small collection and they were never reissued because she considered them the work of a juvenile. In 1921, also, appeared the first book of poems that she was proud to claim authorship of *Nets to Catch the Wind*. This book made her reputation as a poet of great prominence. It won for her the Julia Ellsworth Ford prize that was awarded by the Poetry Society of America for the best book of poems published in the United States in the year 1921. *Black Armour* followed close on the heels of *Nets to Catch the Wind* and this book tended not only to hold her reputation but to increase it. In this second book her expression is more intellectual, and her feeling is more profound. She was more interested in the thought that she had to express than how she should express that thought.

In 1922 her third book of poems came out - *Trivial Breath*. It was written in the same intellectual strain, but her thought is expressed in a more subdued tone and is more variable than in her two preceding books. The contents of her three books to date are just one hundred poems and most of them are quite short. Possibly two or three consist of as many as fifty lines and her longest poem has about two hundred.

Her fourth and last book of poems has been published under the titles of *Angels and Earthly Creatures*. It is so named after the finest poem in the book. It is her heart and not her intellect that speaks through the poems of this collection and they reflect her deeper understanding of herself and of life in general.

When we give careful attention to her four books of poems we invariably conclude that her growth was as sudden as it was remarkable. In the chronological arrangement they show a series of marked advancement.

The proceeding outline of her writings has not included her first four poems, which she called her *First Acceptor*. These were printed in 1820 before her first book *Nets to Catch the Wind* and even these poems are considered as capable of forecasting her master of arts. As she wrote from time to time her poetry gained not only in depth but in simplicity. The outstanding characteristic of all her poetry is clarity and this is noticeable especially in her later poems. Her clarity was the outcome of her carefully striving to attain that end. Although her work was cleverly done, it never seems labored. Peregrine a good example of this:

> Loved a city,
> And street's alarums;
> Parks were pretty
> And so were bar-rooms
> He loved fiddles
> He talked with rustics;
> Life was riddles
> And queer acostics.
>
> The noose draws tighter;
> This is the end;
> I'm a good fighter,
> But a bad friend:
> I've played the traitor
> Over and over;
> I'm a good hater
> But a bad lover.

As a more careful study of her books is made, it may be noted that *Nets to Catch the Wind* does not show the working of a grave and melancholy mind altogether.

There are instances of playfulness and strains of emotion run along through a large number of her poems. She conceieved the idea that our senses are nets which are not strong enough to stop and control the emotions that are all about us and a consequence of this fact we learn but little from our experiences.

CONTENTS

I: BREASTPLATE

Full Moon

My bands of silk and miniver
Momently grew heavier;
The black gauze was beggarly thin;
The ermine muffled mouth and chin;
I could not suck the moonlight in.

Harlequin in lozenges
Of love and hate, I walked in these
Striped and ragged rigmaroles;
Along the pavement my footsoles
Trod warily on living coals.

Shouldering the thoughts I loathed,
In their corrupt disguises clothed,
Mortality I could not tear
From my ribs, to leave them bare
Ivory in silver air.

There I walked, and there I raged;
The spiritual savage caged
Within my skeleton, raged afresh
To feel, behind a carnal mesh,
The clean bones crying in the flesh.

Nebuchadnezzar

My body is weary to death of my mischievous
  brain;
I am weary forever and ever of being brave;
Therefore I crouch on my knees while the cool
  white rain
Curves the clover over my head like a wave.

The stem and the frosty seed of the grass are
  ripe;
I have devoured their strength; I have drunk
  them deep;
And the dandelion is gall in a thin green pipe,
But the clover is honey and sun and the smell
  of sleep.

Three Wishes

Sink out of being, and go down, go down
Through the steep layers of emerald and jade
With warm thin skin of turquoise overlaid,
Where the slow coral spins a ghostly town
Of tower and minaret and fretted crown,
Give up your breath in sleep's subaqueous
    shade,
Hold to oblivion; are you afraid
Of cold deep death? Are you afraid to drown?

You have three flashing looks, like fairy
    wishes;
One burns your eyelids with a lightning-wink
Which turns into a rainbow world, and one
Shows sea-birds brighter than the silver fishes,
And one—the last wild chance before you
    sink—
A flock of dancing clouds about the sun.

Prophecy

I shall lie hidden in a hut
   In the middle of an alder wood,
With the back door blind and bolted shut,
   And the front door locked for good.

I shall lie folded like a saint,
   Lapped in a scented linen sheet,
On a bedstead striped with bright-blue paint,
   Narrow and cold and neat.

The midnight will be glassy black
   Behind the panes, with wind about
To set his mouth against a crack
   And blow the candle out.

Epitaph

For this she starred her eyes with salt
And scooped her temples thin,
Until her face shone pure of fault
From the forehead to the chin.

In coldest crucibles of pain
Her shrinking flesh was fired
And smoothed into a finer grain
To make it more desired.

Pain left her lips more clear than glass;
It colored and cooled her hand.
She lay a field of scented grass
Yielded as pasture land.

For this her loveliness was curved
And carved as silver is:
For this she was brave: but she deserved
A better grave than this.

[16]

Song

It is my thoughts that colour
My soul which slips between;
Thoughts lunar and solar
And gold and sea-green

Tint the pure translucence
Of the crystal thread;
A rainbow nuisance
It runs through my head.

When I am dead, or sleeping
Without any pain,
My soul will stop creeping
Through my jewelled brain.

With no brightness to dye it
None will see where
It flows clear and quiet
As a river of air;

Watering dark places
Without sparkle or sound;
Kissing dumb faces
And the dusty ground.

Drowned Woman

He shall be my jailer
Who sets me free
From shackles frailer
Than the wind-spun sea.

He shall be my teacher
Who cries "Be brave."
To a weeping creature
In a glass-walled wave.

But he shall be my brother
Whose mocking despair
Dives headlong to smother
In the weeds of my hair.

The Good Birds

Threading the evil hand and look
I sprang, on sinews spare and light,
To sleep beside a water-brook
Where snow was sprinkled overnight.

I spread my cloak upon the ground,
I laid my head upon a stone,
I stared into the sky and found
That I no longer lived alone.

He turned His burning eyes on me
From smoke above a mountain-shelf;
I did not want His company
Who wanted no one but myself.

I whistled shrill, I whistled keen;
The birds were servant to my nod.
They wove their wings into a screen
Between my lovely ground and God.
[20]

II: GAUNTLET

Peregrine

Liar and bragger,
He had no friend
Except a dagger
And a candle-end;
The one he read by;
The one scared cravens;
And he was fed by
The Prophet's ravens.
Such haughty creatures
Avoid the human;
They fondle nature's
Breast, not woman—
A she-wolf's puppies—
A wild-cat's pussy-fur:
Their stirrup-cup is
The pride of Lucifer.
A stick he carried,
Slept in a lean-to;

He'd never married,
And he didn't mean to.
He'd tried religion
And found it pleasant;
He relished a pigeon
Stewed with a pheasant
In an iron kettle;
He built stone ovens.
He'd never settle
In any province.
He made pantries
Of Vaux and Arden
And the village gentry's
Kitchen-garden.
Fruits within yards
Were his staples;
He drank whole vineyards
From Rome to Naples,
Then went to Brittany
For the cider.
He could sit any
Horse, a rider
Outstripping Cheiron's
Canter and gallop.

Pau's environs
The pubs of Salop,
Wells and Bath inns
Shared his pleasure
With taverns of Athens;
The Sultan's treasure
He'd seen in Turkey;
He'd known London
Bright and murky.
His bones were sunned on
Paris benches
Beset by sparrows;
Roman trenches,
Cave-men's barrows,
He liked, impartial;
He liked an Abbey.
His step was martial;
Spent and shabby
He wasn't broken;
A dozen lingoes
He must have spoken.
As a king goes
He went, not minding
That he lived seeking

And never finding.
He'd visit Peking
And then be gone soon
To the far Canaries;
He'd cross a monsoon
To chase vagaries.
He loved a city
And a street's alarums;
Parks were pretty
And so were bar-rooms.
He loved fiddles;
He talked with rustics;
Life was riddles
And queer acrostics.
His sins were serried,
His virtues garish;
His corpse was buried
In a country parish.
Before he went hence—
God knows where—
He spoke this sentence
With a princely air:
"The noose draws tighter;
This is the end;

I'm a good fighter,
But a bad friend:
I've played the traitor
Over and over;
. I'm a good hater,
But a bad lover."

Heroics

Though here and there a man is left
Whose iron thread eludes the shears,
The martyr with his bosom cleft
Is dead these seven heavy years.

Does he survive whose tongue was slit,
To slake some envy of a king's?
Sportive silver cried from it
Before the savage cut the strings.

The rack has crumpled up the limb
Stretched immediate to fly;
Never ask the end of him
Stubborn to outstare the sky.

Assuming an heroic mask,
He stands a tall derisive tree,
While servile to the speckled task
We move devoted hand and knee.

[28]

It is no virtue, but a fault
Thus to breathe ignoble air,
Suffering unclean assault
And insult dubious to bear.

Lucifer Sings in Secret

I am the broken arrow
From Jehovah's quiver;
He will not let me sorrow
Forever and ever.
He will give me a new feather
That is white, not red;
He will bind me together
With the hairs of his head.
My shaft will be jointed
Like the young springing corn;
My tip will be pointed
With a painted thorn.
He will be willing
That I lift my voice,
Among all killing
To make my choice;
To harry the wagons
Of the wicked's retreat;

To murder dragons
Who have licked my feet.
I shall choose the target
His arrow deserves;
I shall trace and mark it
In scarlet curves.
Small and bloody
As a fallen sparrow
My own dead body
Shall receive his arrow.

Preference

These to me are beautiful people;
Thick hair sliding in a ripple;
A tall throat, round as a column;
A mournful mouth, small and solemn,
Having to confound the mourner
Irony in either corner;
The limbs fine, narrow and strong;
Like the wind they walk along,
Like the whirlwind, bad to follow;
The cheekbones high, the cheeks hollow,
The eyes large and wide apart.
They carry a dagger in the heart
So keen and clean it never rankles. . . .
They wear small bones in wrists and ankles.

Simon Gerty

(Who Turned Renegade and Lived With the Indians)

By what appalling dim upheaval
  Demolishing some kinder plan,
Did you become incarnate evil
  Wearing the livery of man?

Perhaps you hated cheeks of tallow,
  Dead eyes, and lineaments of chalk,
Until a beauty came to hallow
  Even the bloodiest tomahawk.

Perhaps you loathed your brothers' features
  Pallid and pinched, or greasy-fat;
Perhaps you loved these alien creatures
  Clean muscled as a panther cat.

Did you believe that being cruel
  Was that which made their foreheads lift
So proudly, gave their eyes a jewel,
  And turned their padding footsteps swift?

[33]

As one by one our faiths are shaken
Our hatreds fall; so mine for you.
Of course I think you were mistaken;
But still, I see your point of view.

Let No Charitable Hope

Now let no charitable hope
Confuse my mind with images
Of eagle and of antelope:
I am in nature none of these.

I was, being human, born alone;
I am, being woman, hard beset;
I live by squeezing from a stone
The little nourishment I get.

In masks outrageous and austere
The years go by in single file;
But none has merited my fear,
And none has quite escaped my smile.

This Hand

This hand you have observed,
Impassive and detached,
With joints adroitly curved,
And fingers neatly matched:

Blue-veined and yellowish,
Ambiguous to clasp,
And secret as a fish,
And sudden as an asp:

It doubles to a fist,
Or droops composed and chill;
The socket of my wrist
Controls it to my will.

It leaps to my command,
Tautened, or trembling lax;
It lies within your hand
Anatomy of wax.

[36]

If I had seen a thorn
Broken to grape vine bud;
If I had ever borne
Child of our mingled blood;

Elixirs might escape;
But now, compact as stone,
My hand preserves a shape
Too utterly its own.

III: HELMET

Self-Portrait

A lens of crystal whose transparence calms
Queer stars to clarity, and disentangles
Fox-fires to form austere refracted angles:
A texture polished on the horny palms
Of vast equivocal creatures, beast or human:
A flint, a substance finer-grained than snow,
Graved with the Graces in intaglio
To set sarcastic sigil on the woman.

This for the mind, and for the little rest
A hollow scooped to blackness in the breast,
The simulacrum of a cloud, a feather:
Instead of stone, instead of sculptured strength,
This soul, this vanity, blown hither and
    thither
By trivial breath, over the whole world's
    length.

Cold Blooded Creatures

Man, the egregious egoist,
(In mystery the twig is bent,)
Imagines, by some mental twist,
That he alone is sentient

Of the intolerable load
Which on all living creatures lies,
Nor stoops to pity in the toad
The speechless sorrow of its eyes.

He asks no questions of the snake,
Nor plumbs the phosphorescent gloom
Where lidless fishes, broad awake,
Swim staring at a night-mare doom.

King Honour's Eldest Son

His father's steel, piercing the wholesome fruit
Of his mother's flesh, wrought acidly to mar
Its own Damascus, staining worse than war
A purity intense and absolute;
While her clean stock put forth a poisoned
    shoot,
In likeness of a twisted scimitar,
Sleek as a lovelock, ugly as a scar,
Wrong as the firstborn of a mandrake root.

There was a waning moon upon his brow,
A fallen star upon his pointed chin;
He mingled Ariel with Caliban;
But such a blossom upon such a bough
Convinced his poor progenitors of sin
In having made a something more than man.

Nonchalance

This cool and laughing mind, renewed
From covert sources like a spring's,
Is potent to translate the mood
Of all distraught and twisted things.

In this clear water shall be cast
Outrageous shapes of steel and gold,
And all their hot and clotted past
Beaded with bubbles silver-cold.

The moving power takes their heat
Into itself, forgetting them;
And warmth in trickles, slow and sweet
Comforts a fainting lily-stem.

South

Spotted by sun, and visible
Above me in a wave-green vault,
With that thick sticky linden-smell
Saturate, as the sea with salt.

Transmuting all the blue to green
And all the green to serpents' tongues,
Deep, ponderable, felt and seen,
And breathed in pain, with heavy lungs.

Is this that limber element
Which runs like light, and will not stop
To drink the apple's sap and scent
While thirsting for the mountain-top?

Demon Lovers

The peacock and the mocking-bird
Cry forever in her breast;
Public libraries have blurred
The pages of his palimpsest.

He wanders lonely as a cloud
In chevelure of curled perruque;
Masked assassins in a crowd
Strangle the uxorious duke.

Castilian facing Lucifer,
Juan does not remove his cap;
Unswaddled infantile to her
His soul lies kicking in her lap.

While she, transported by the wind,
Mercutio has clasped and kissed. . . .
Like quicksilver, her absent mind
Evades them both, and is not missed.

[46]

Fable

A knight lay dead in Senlac:
One white raven stood
Where his breast-bone showed a crack:
She dipped her beak in blood.

The old man's lean and carven head
Was severed under the chin:
The raven's beak was varnished red
Where the veins ran small and thin.

Empty sockets sucked the light
Where the great gold eyes had shone:
Oh, but the raven's eyes were bright
With fire she supped upon!

The old man's beard was ravelled up
In stiff and webby skeins:
From his broad skull's broken cup
The raven sipped his brains.

[47]

Insensate with that burning draught
Her feathers turned to flame:
Like a cruel silver shaft
Across the sun she came.

She flew straight into God's house;
She drank the virtuous air.
A knight lay dead: his gutted brows
Gaped hollow under his hair.

IV: BEAVER UP

Castilian

Velasquez took a pliant knife
And scraped his palette clean;
He said, "I lead a dog's own life
Painting a king and queen."

He cleaned his palette with oily rags
And oakum from Seville wharves;
"I am sick of painting painted hags
And bad ambiguous dwarves.

"The sky is silver, the clouds are pearl,
Their locks are looped with rain.
I will not paint Maria's girl
For all the money in Spain."

He washed his face in water cold,
His hands in turpentine;
He squeezed out colour like coins of gold
And colour like drops of wine.

Each colour lay like a little pool
On the polished cedar wood;
Clear and pale and ivory-cool
Or dark as solitude.

He burnt the rags in the fireplace
And leaned from the window high;
He said, "I like that gentleman's face
Who wears his cap awry."

This is the gentleman, there he stands,
Castilian, sombre-caped,
With arrogant eyes, and narrow hands
Miraculously shaped.

Sequence

I

This is the end of all, and yet I strive
To fight for nothing, having nothing kept
Of loveliness that saved myself alive
Before this killing distillation crept
Numbing my limbs, and stiffening my tongue
To clay, less vital than the salted thorn
Whereon a tyrant's banneret is hung
As scarecrow for a harvesting still-born:
And I am barren in a barren land,
But who so breaks me, I shall pierce his hand.

This much is true, that there were certain times,
Measured by minutes, with a blank between,
When our two courages could meet, and climb
Into the blue above the blowing green;
But now the lifted pasture is too high,
The shoal too deep, for such were noble graves;
In this unlighted kennel, where to die

Will not awaken hounds, nor anger slaves,
I shall advise me to prepare my couch;
Here it is dark; for more I may not vouch.

II

One of these men will find my skeleton;
To one it will be delicate and slim,
With stars for eyes, and portent of a sun
Rising between the ribs to frighten him;
Yet, being bold, he might embrace it soon
With quick insensate passion in the night,
And by the holy taper of the moon
Encouraged, and because its bones were light
As filagree of pearl, he might depart
Bearing my jangled heart-strings on his heart.

And he might bury it in sand or sod,
Stamping it down to circumvent the wolf,
And, being kind, commend it to his God,
Whose Mind was swimming somewhere in the
    gulf
Above his head; but if that other found
The rotten framework of his servitor,
He'd leave it lying on the cluttered ground
Between a bottle and an apple-core,

[54]

And go his way, in agony and sweat,
Because he could not pity nor forget.

III

For various questions which I shall not ask,
And various answers which I cannot hear,
I have contrived a substituted task
To prove my body is devoid of fear;
To prove my spirit's elemental blood
Is pure, courageous, and uniform,
I shall submerge my body in the mud,
I shall submit my spirit to the storm;
I shall bend down my bosom to the snake,
As to an infant for its father's sake.

I shall persist, I shall pursue my way
Believing that his cruelty was fine
As tempered steel for chastening of clay,
Impatient of corrosions that were mine;
He that despised me shall not be forgot;
He that disparaged me shall be my lord;
That was a flambeau, half-consumed and hot,
This was the running light along a sword;
And though I warmed my fingers at the one,
The other is my father and my son.

[55]

Little Sonnet

Let your loving bondwoman
Salute your lips if you prefer;
This is your courtesy to her.
Yet still remember how she ran
From her grave, and running, leapt
To catch the arrows of your hurt,
To stretch her body in dust and dirt,
Flinging a causey where you stepped.

Remember how, asleep or waking,
The shallow pillow of her breast
Shook and shook to your heart's shaking,
In pity whereof her heart was split;
Love her now; forget the rest;
She has herself forgotten it.

[56]

Pity Me

Pity the wolves who prowl unsleeping
  Guarding the pasture from a thief;
Pity the proud leopards weeping
  Tears of subtle grief.

Pity the savage panthers sheathing
  Sharp disdain in silken gloves;
Pity the golden lions breathing
  Fire upon their loves.

Pity the prickly star that frightens
  The Christ Child with its shattered spear;
Pity the midnight when it lightens;
  Pity me, my dear.

Unfinished Portrait

My love, you know that I have never used
That fluency of colour smooth and rich
Could cage you in enamel for the niche
Whose heart-shape holds you; I have been
    accused
Of gold and silver trickery, infused
With blood of meteors, and moonstones which
Are cold as eyeballs in a flooded ditch;
In no such goblin smithy are you bruised.

I do not glaze a lantern like a shell
Inset with stars, nor make you visible
Through jewelled arabesques which adhere to
    clothe
The outline of your soul; I am content
To leave you an uncaptured element;
Water, or light, or air that's stained by both

[58]

Benvenuto's Valentine

Not for the child that wanders home
So wasted by barbaric kings,
So wearied by imperial Rome,
That he will clasp my apron-strings.

Not for the ghost that never is
And never will be known by me,
Whose heel is on the precipice
Before its print has left the sea.

And not for darling Harlequin
Spinning in stars of diamond shape;
Nor Hamlet exquisite and thin
As moonbeams in an inky cape.

Not for the legend latest-born
Of Chivalry and Virgin, whom
Roland has knighted with a horn,
And Richard with a sprig of broom.

Not even for the man who climbed
A thousand miles to thrust a torch
Among forgotten fagots, rimed
By winter in an iron porch.

But for the thought, that wrought and planned
Such intricate and crystal things,
My kiss is set upon your hand
As softly as a silver ring's.

Twelfth Night

It has always been King Herod that I feared;
　King Herod and his kinsmen, ever since. . . .
I do not like the colour of your beard;
　I think that you are wicked, and a prince.

I keep no stable . . . how your horses stamp! . . .
　If you are wise men, you will leave me soon;
I have been frightened by a thievish tramp
　Who counted bloody silver in the moon.

You get no lodging underneath these roofs,
　No, though you pay in frankincense and
　　myrrh;
Your harness jangles with your horses' hooves;
　Be quiet; you will wake him if you stir.

This is no church for Zoroastrians,
　Nor resting-place for governors from Rome;
Oh, I have knowledge of your secret plans;
　Your faces are familiar; go home.

And you, young captain of the lion stare,
    Subdue your arrogance to this advice;
You should forbid your soldiery to swear,
    To spit at felons, and to play at dice.

You have perceived, above the chimney ledge,
    Hanging inverted by Saint David's harp,
His sword from heaven, with the double edge
    Which, for your service, is no longer sharp.

He sleeps, like some ingenuous shepherd boy
    Or carpenter's apprentice, but his slim
And wounded hands shall never more destroy
    Another giant; do not waken him.

The counterpane conceals the deeper wound
    Which lately I have washed with vinegar;
Now let this iron bar be importuned;
    I say you shall not speak to him of war.

V: PLUMES

Now That Your Eyes Are Shut

Now that your eyes are shut
Not even a dusty butterfly may brush them;
My flickering knife has cut
Life from sonorous lion throats to hush them.

If pigeons croon too loud
Or lambs bleat proudly, they must come to
    slaughter,
And I command each cloud
To be precise in spilling silent water.

Let light forbear those lids;
I have forbidden the feathery ash to smutch
    them;
The spider thread that thrids
The gray-plumed grass has not my leave to
    touch them.

My casual ghost may slip,
Issuing tiptoe, from the pure inhuman;
The tissues of my lip
Will bruise your eyelids, while I am a woman.

Lilliputian

She hoards green cheeses
On a high moonlight shelf;
Her tea-kettle freezes;
The child is an elf.

Her shiny mind is peopled
By brisk goblins, but
Though castled and steepled
The place is Lilliput:

Where I lie bound by subtle
Spider-web and hair,
And the small feet scuttle,
And the gold eyes stare.

Parting Gift

I cannot give you the Metropolitan Tower;
I cannot give you heaven;
Nor the nine Visigoth crowns in the Cluny
    Museum;
Nor happiness, even.
But I can give you a very small purse
Made out of field-mouse skin,
With a painted picture of the universe
And seven blue tears therein.

I cannot give you the island of Capri;
I cannot give you beauty;
Nor bake you marvelous crusty cherry pies
With love and duty.
But I can give you a very little locket
Made out of wildcat hide:
Put it into your left-hand pocket
And never look inside.

[68]

Francie's Fingers

"Oh, Francie, sell me your fingers
And I will pay you well!"
Sweet flowed that voice, the singer's,
As gillyflowers smell.

"Your fingers are a witch's,
White as china clay,
Thin as willow switches
Pointed up to pray.

"For your dinted knuckles
And blue printed wrist
I'll give you my buckles
Of paste and amethyst."

"I will sell my fingers
If you will sell your tongue;
Your voice is a singer's
Whose veins run song.

"If apples sprang from heaven
Instead of from the ground,
Their juice could not even
Be sweet as that sound."

"Oh, sell your smallest finger!"
"Your voice is all I fancy!"
"No, no!" replied the singer.
"Oh, no, no!" cried Francie.

Beware!

To Baba, Playing a Nocturne by Chopin

Baba flourishes and dips,
Little gestures poise and gleam;
Now her shiny finger-tips
Strike the surface of the stream.

Now she plunges both her wrists
In the water blue as air,
Curdling into starry mists,
Diapered with light despair.

Deep above the drowning sands
Sorrow like a moon is drowned;
Baba, only dip your hands
In the surface of the sound.

Gifts at Meeting
From the Greek

Violets, sparsely
Budded, to wreathe
With sprigs of parsley;
A kid to seethe
In its own juices
Dilute with wine;
Sweetmeats from cruises
Transpontine;
A sapling, studded
With apricocks,
Cream, new-crudded,
Butter in crocks;
A barrel of tunny,
A barley bun;
Combs of honey
That smell like the sun:
Plaited withies

Piled with white grapes;
From Persian smithies
Smooth dagger-shapes;
Cups of lapis
And mirrors of bronze;
Springes, to trap us
Geese and swans;
A wild deer's haunches
And a lion's head;
Coral branches
Silver and red;
A pirate's earring
And a painted book,
I bring you, fearing
Your blackthorn crook.

To Aphrodite, with a Talisman

This graven charm, that leads a girl unkissed
From bridal-bed; that knows to draw a man
Far over-seas; carved out of amethyst,
Chased with fine gold; accept, O Cyprian!

See where it lies, translucent, beautiful:
Oh, take it for your very own! and see
How it is bound with violet-coloured wool,
Gift of a sorceress from Thessaly.

To a Blackbird Singing
Marcus Argentarius

Where the poisonous mistletoe
Over the oak her magic weaves,
Sing no more, O blackbird! go
To safer shade of silver leaves.

Sing, and set your little foot
On golden grape and silver vine:
The Wine-God loves your song: the fruit
Will cool your lovely throat with wine.

On a Singing Girl

Musa of the sea-blue eyes,
Silver nightingale, alone
In a little coffin lies:
A stone beneath a stone.

She, whose song we loved the best,
Is voiceless in a sudden night:
On your light limbs, O loveliest,
May the dust be light!

To Claudia Homonoea

My words were delicately breathed
As Syren notes: the Cyprian's head
Never shone out more golden-wreathed
Than mine: but now I lie here dead.

A chattering swallow, bright and wild,
Whom one man loved for all her years—
Having loved her even as a child:
I leave him nothing but his tears.

Printed in Great Britain
by Amazon

30984401R00047